*pocket guides*

# COMBS and
# HAIR ACCESSORIES

by

Norma Hague

*Series Editor:* Noël Riley

**SEVEN HILLS BOOKS**
Cincinnati

**LUTTERWORTH PRESS**
Cambridge

Cover illustration shows a silver-gilt filigree comb
with turquoises and enamel, Indian workmanship *c*.1870–80
(photo, Eric Shenton).

*To Norma Warnock*

**First published in 1985 by Lutterworth Press,
7 All Saints' Passage, Cambridge CB2 3LS.**
U.K. ISBN 0–7188–2593–4

Published in the United States by Seven Hills Books,
519 West Third Street, Cincinnati, Oh. 45202.
U.S. ISBN 0–911403–11–6

Photoset by Nene Phototypesetters Ltd, Northampton

Printed and bound in Great Britain by Butler & Tanner Ltd
Frome and London

# Contents

1. Mid-Victorian tiara comb, electrogilt metal. The design and heavy appearance are typical of ornaments 1860–1880.

# Introduction

THE practice of decorating the hair itself, as distinct from the wearing of elaborate head-dress, first came into vogue in the second half of the 16th century. It became the custom for upper-class women to wear little or no head-covering, and to adorn their complex coiffures with decorative accessories. In this, they were following the example set by Queen Elizabeth I, whose portraits are a rich source of information for late 16th century hair ornaments and coiffure. In the succeeding centuries, hair accessories enjoyed fluctuating fortunes, according to the nature of the fashion and hairstyle of the time. However, it should be remembered that the uncovered head, and its adornment with jewels and ornaments, was predominantly an

2. Diamond aigrette of flowers and wheatears design, set in silver and gold, English or French, late 18th century.

aristocratic habit. By custom, respectable middle-class women invariably wore a cap of some kind, even with their 'best' clothes. In the late 18th century the dress-cap became a mere pouf of gauze surmounting the formal dressing, and the use of decorative accessories in the hair itself became the accepted mode for court and society. The Neoclassical movement brought 'Greek' costumes and coiffures into fashion from 1795, and the use of ornaments to adorn the hair soon became widespread among the middle-classes.

The collecting of these accessories today is a relatively unexplored field and, so far, little has been written of them. The accessories covered here date from the mid-18th century up to about 1940. Ornaments of an earlier date are museum pieces now, and outside the scope of the average collector. Likewise, the emphasis here is not upon priceless diamond tiaras, but upon ornaments of a more modest nature. Primary jewels, set with diamonds and valuable stones, were designed to serve through several generations, and were mostly conservative in design. Those in less costly materials could be more innovative, reflecting changing tastes and new discoveries. They were not intended to last beyond the immediate fashion. Nevertheless, many have survived in excellent condition, and are widely available to the present-day collector.

# 1.    Georgian to Romantic, 1760–1840

3. The hair dressed over pads, ornamented with pearls and an aigrette. *Lady's Magazine*, May, 1773.

BY the second half of the 18th century a clear distinction had evolved between formal and informal dress. For everyday, the coiffure was often simple, and covered by a lace or muslin cap. However, for court wear and other splendid occasions, it was customary for women to powder their hair, and to adorn it elaborately. The trend was towards greater height as the century advanced, and this was achieved by raising the hair over pads. The whole was powdered, and dressed with ornaments of gauze, jewels, ropes of pearls, or tall ostrich plumes, according to fancy. Some extreme coiffures in the 1770s were even arranged to represent a ship at sea, or a rural landscape with animals! Although only a small minority of ultra-fashionable women adopted such outlandish coiffures, many still followed the trend towards increased height, and the lavish use of decorative accessories (fig. 3).

Technical advances in the art of gem-cutting now enabled the unique optical properties of the diamond to be better displayed, and these gems came to the fore in Georgian jewellery design. Diamonds were, therefore, the stones chiefly employed in such accessories as diadems, bandeaux and hairpins. Some

4. *(below)* Aigrette in cockade form, gold with foiled garnets, late 18th century.

7

5. Garnet and gold aigrette with tremblant butterfly, bow and leaf motif, English *c*.1760.

6. Garnet and gold aigrette in typical Georgian design of tremblant bird on a spray, English *c*.1760.

jewels at this period could be used interchangeably in a number of ways – sewn to the dress, mounted on a velvet band for neckwear, or pinned into the hair. However, there were still important accessories designed exclusively for wear in the hair. Of these, the aigrette is probably the most typical hair ornament of the late 18th century. This is an upstanding decoration, usually in the form of a feather or flower-spray, intended to be worn at the side of the high coiffure, and to rise above it. Late 18th century motifs also made use of bows, crescents, wheat-ears, and flowers in the construction of aigrettes (figs. 2 and 4). The diamonds were in an open, or *à jour* setting of gold or silver. Sometimes, coloured stones such as topaz, amethysts or garnets might be employed, or pastes coloured to simulate them (fig. 7). When using pastes or coloured gemstones it was the custom to place each stone in a closed setting backed by a small piece of foil, in order to improve the colour and reflective qualities. This method gave way to the claw setting in the early 19th century, and is a helpful consideration when recognizing Georgian pieces. An attractive feature of many aigrettes is that an important element – a flower, butterfly or bird – is made *tremblant*, that is, placed on a spring or flexible wire so that it quivers with every movement of the wearer's head (figs. 5 and 6). At this period, of course, rooms were lit by candlelight, which would have shed a softly-diffused glow on all

7. *(above)* Crescent and spray aigrette, pastes in a closed-back setting, English or French, late 18th century.

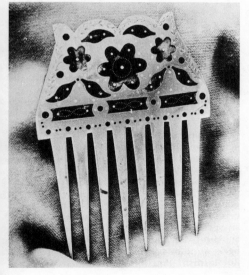

8. Brass comb with tortoiseshell and silver piqué inlay, possibly English, mid-18th century.

9. An important early steel back-comb with blue and white Wedgwood jasperware cameos, English c.1785–90.

10. (below) Empire hairdressing showing the use of ornamental net, bandeau with cameos, and an upstanding comb. *Journal für Luxus*, July, 1812.

these glittering ornaments. In addition to aigrettes, various other gem-set stars, butterflies, bows and crescents might be mounted upon two-pronged pins and scattered about the formal dressing. Today, collectors may well come across such Georgian accessories which were later converted into brooches or pendants.

An important aspect of late 18th and 19th century ornaments, and one which favours the modest collector, is the emergence of jewellery in secondary materials. The Industrial Revolution brought about the rise of a prosperous middle-class who, if they could not emulate the gold and diamonds of the aristocracy, could certainly afford ornaments set with less expensive gemstones or fine-quality pastes (fig. 7). A substitute for gold came in the form of pinchbeck, an alloy of copper and zinc which does not tarnish. Pinchbeck, decorated with cut-

11. Three silver-gilt haircombs, c.1800–20.

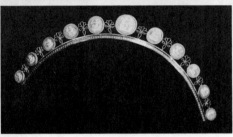

12. Pinchbeck tiara with graduated shell cameos, English or French, 1800–10.

steel or pastes was widely used for this, the first true costume jewellery. Many of these Georgian hair accessories in paste, cut-steel and pinchbeck have survived because of the excellence of their workmanship. Also, being of low intrinsic value, they were not broken up, like some more expensive jewels.

Another traditional accessory for the hair, and one which remained in use throughout the whole of the period covered here, is the decorative hair comb. Its chief vogue dates from about 1795, although combs were certainly worn before this. These early ornamental combs were made mostly from inexpensive materials such as carved and pierced horn, tortoiseshell with piqué (gold or silver inlay), gilded silver, or polished steel (figs. 8, 9). A feature to notice when dating combs is that these early examples are often flat in construction, rather than deeply curved to the head, as

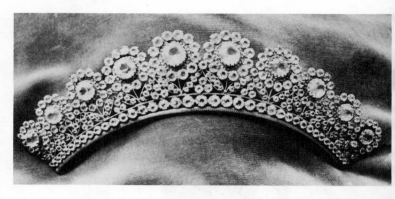

13. *(above)* Pinchbeck tiara with pastes in openwork floral design, English or French, 1800–20.

14. *(below)* Silver filigree comb with classical motifs of feathers and grapes, English, Birmingham 1806.

in later ornaments. The idea of shaping both prongs and heading to give a comfortable fit seems to have evolved gradually. However, as women's hairstyles were still fairly voluminous in the late 18th century, a large degree of shaping would not have been required to make them comfortable.

By 1795, the fashionable coiffure had passed its extreme of height, and the neoclassical influence began to affect the style of dress. The fashionable line was based on that of ancient Greece, with a high waistline placed directly below the breasts. The comparative simplicity of these gowns was compensated for by the highly ornamental coiffures, which imitated those of antiquity. The usual form was a mass of curls or chignon encircled by a diadem, or jewelled or cameo-set bandeau in the Grecian style (fig. 10).

The low neckline and high waist of empire gowns concentrated attention upon the head and shoulders, so that accessories for the hair became one of the most important elements in formal costume. With these gowns, splendid parures, or sets of jewellery were worn, and they usually included a tiara or diadem, placed low on the brow. Often, a matching comb was thrust into the high chignon in such a way as to be visible from all angles (fig. 11). The aristocracy could commission the most splendid

15. Berlin-iron comb mount with cameos, each mounted on a polished steel ground, probably French, c.1800–20.

16. Silver-gilt tiara formed as a laurel wreath, 1800–20.

gem-set parures, while less affluent women made do with tiaras and combs in inexpensive materials, many of which have survived. Diadems of silver-gilt decorated with cameos, seed-pearls, coral or agates were available in a whole range of 'classical' motifs (fig. 12). On a more modest scale though nevertheless pleasing are diadems of pinchbeck or fire-gilt metal, adorned with pastes coloured to simulate precious stones (fig. 13). Despite their slight intrinsic worth, these hair accessories are almost invariably of good workmanship, and display a wide range of designs.

In tune with the popular taste for pale colours and flimsy muslin ball-gowns, the hair accessories of the period are often light and delicate in appearance. The motifs used were based upon those of antiquity – vine leaves, clusters of grapes (fig. 14), the Greek key pattern, and classical portrait heads (fig. 15). One of the most attractive neoclassical ornaments was a diadem of gold or silver-gilt formed as a wreath of laurel (fig. 16). On

13

17. Silver-gilt filigree floral comb, probably French, *c.*1800–20.

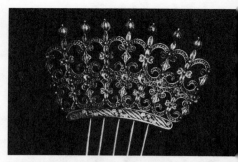

18. Combs in silver-gilt filigree (*left*), and seed-pearls (*right*), possibly French, 1800–10.

occasion, berries might be added in enamel, pearls or coral. Bandeau ornaments of gold set with cameos, cut-steel, or pinchbeck adorned with pastes were set low on the brow in the approved classical manner.

A form of jewellery particularly in keeping with the diaphanous textiles was filigree, either of gold or silver, which was widely used for both combs and diadems in the early 19th century. The medium was well-suited to the high back-combs which were worn at the Napoleonic court, as well as the more restrained examples found in English wear. The usual motifs employed were scrollwork, flowers (fig. 17), feathers, or clusters of grapes (fig. 14). Often too, the headings of such combs show an asymmetric tendency, with the design inclined to one side. These combs were adorned with cameos of shell or Wedgwood jasperware (fig. 9), agates, coral or seed-pearls

19. Elaborate cut-steel tiara, English c.1820–30.

20. Comb of *Peigne Josephine* type with knobs covered by steel beads, French, 1820–40.

(fig. 18), employing all the 'classical' designs already mentioned.

Two interesting materials employed for hair accessories at this period were cut-steel and Berlin-iron. The former consists of hand-faceted steel studs riveted on to a metal backing-plate, and massed together to form flower, rosette, leaf and star patterns (figs. 19, 20). The effect, when the highly-polished steel studs caught the light, was one of richness and glitter. Berlin-iron is a much more sombre material, and hair ornaments in this medium are rarer (figs. 15 and 37). Tradition has it that when the Germans were fighting against Napoleon, the government urged the aristocracy to sacrifice their jewels for the war effort. Those who did so were rewarded with ornaments of cast-iron in neoclassical designs. Some were even inscribed with patriotic mottoes such as *Gold gab ich für Eisen* ('I gave gold

21. *(above)* Silver-gilt 'arrow' pins set with foiled pastes, English or French, 1800–40.

for iron'). The fashion for Berlin-iron caught the public imagination, and out-lasted Napoleon by many years, spreading throughout Europe.

Another hair accessory typical of the opening years of the 19th century is a pin in the form of an arrow, about six to eight inches in length (fig. 21). This was used to pierce the high chignon or topknot, and several might be worn at one time. One end was sharply pointed to pierce the hair, and the other decorated in various ways to form an ornamental top. The designs vary from open-work flowers to butterflies, set with pearls, garnets, turquoise, or coloured pastes. These attractive little ornaments are generally found nowadays converted into brooches, since they are unwearable in their original form. In the shape of arrows and daggers, such pins re-

22. Elaborate coiffure with false 'Apollo' knots, tortoiseshell comb, and typical forehead ornament (*ferronnière*). *Petit Courrier des Dames*, 1829.

mained fashionable and were worn until the early 1840s.

In the late 1820s the fashionable coiffure and the accessories used to adorn it had become extremely complex. Great stiffened loops of hair, often false, and known as Apollo knots, were placed on the crown to give height to the dressing (fig. 22). The base of the knots was encircled by some form of ornament, such as a wreath of flowers or laurel leaves, as well as bandeaux, and tiara-like ornaments. Important accessories were the long pins, known as Glauvina pins. These were produced in a wide range of materials and designs, with jewelled tops in the form of stars, flowers, butterflies, arrows, and so on. They were placed in such a way as to protrude some inches from the head, and several were worn at a time (fig. 23).

There was a great liking for *tremblant* ornaments of all kinds, either as jewelled sprigs, aigrettes, or the aforementioned hairpins. A favourite motif for this purpose was a butterfly

23. *(above)* Elaborate hairpins in gold and semi-precious stones, 1830–40.

24. *(below)* Butterfly hairpins in various materials.

25. Set of interchangeable seed-pearl hair ornaments in the shapes of birds, flowers and a crescent, English, 1820–30.

placed on a flexible wire, so that it appeared to hover over the wearer's head (fig. 24). In other ornaments stars or flowers were likewise placed upon quivering wires. Among the most attractive ornaments of this type are those of seed-pearls (fig. 25). In this form of jewellery, minute pearls are sewn with horsehair on to a backing of mother-of-pearl so as to form various designs, mainly floral, although birds, stars and crescents are also common. These seed-pearl ornaments were considered particularly suitable for young girls, probably because of their chaste and delicate appearance. There was also a definite etiquette which governed the wearing of jewellery. The most valuable gemstones were the perquisite of married women, while materials of small intrinsic worth, such as seed-pearls, turquoise, coral and ivory were thought better suited to young ladies.

Acting partly as a support for the loops of

26. *(above)* Large pierced back-comb in fire-gilt brass. Height (excluding prongs), 8 in. French or Spanish, 1828–35.

27. Back-comb in dark tortoiseshell with openwork design. Height (excluding prongs) 10 in. English or French, *c*.1828–35.

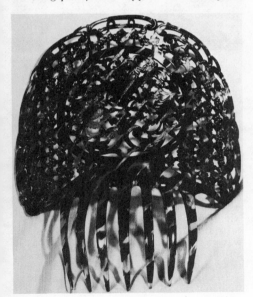

19

28. Pinchbeck and cut-steel bandeau with butterfly motifs, English 1830–45.

29. Diamond tiara of foliate scrolls and flowerheads, early 19th century.

hair, paradise plumes, and formidable hairpins, many coiffures also had a high Spanish-style back-comb placed at the rear of the dressing. In some of these combs the heading might be as much as eight or ten inches in height, so that the form of decoration would be visible from all angles (figs. 26 and 27). Pierced openwork patterns, usually floral or scrolled and often of lace-like delicacy, were among the most favoured. Some of these combs were in pinchbeck or filigree metal, but by far the most popular material for them was tortoiseshell, of which the blond variety was preferred. In the early 19th century the making of these combs was still a handicraft. Horn was also used, although tortoiseshell was a considerably more expensive material. Most horn combs were, therefore, treated with chemicals to simulate the surface markings of the more

30. Silver-gilt scrollwork tiara set with turquoise, 1840–55.

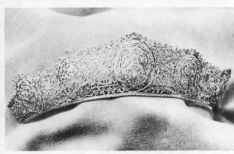

31. Tiara of openwork in two-colour gold, French 1830–50.

desirable shell. This was often very cunningly done, so that it is difficult now to determine which is genuine.

By the early 1830s the high elaborate coiffures had subsided in favour of a flat-topped dressing, with a small chignon, or a series of loops placed at the crown. The high back-combs disappeared, along with the styles they had sustained, and their place was taken by head-encircling accessories of various kinds. Bandeaux, worn across the forehead or placed at the hairline were a favourite ornament, and appeared in a wide range of materials and designs. The preferred motifs for their decoration were flowers, butterflies (fig. 28) or stars set with coloured stones, pastes or cut-steel. Tiaras were mostly small and light, formed of openwork set with pearls or turquoise, or filigree (figs. 29, 30 and 31).

32. Silver-gilt comb with engraved 'Renaissance' heading and garnets inset, English, 1840–55.

AT the beginning of Queen Victoria's reign the hair was usually parted in the centre, and drawn back into a coiled or plaited chignon on the crown, or lower. This was an era of great nostalgic interest in the past, and there developed a taste for ornaments in the styles of the middle ages and Renaissance. In hair accessories, these influences appear in indirect ways – by the revival of such lapsed jewellery techniques as granulation, filigree and enamel – rather than by exact copies of early head-ornaments. Small tiaras and ornamental combs in gold and silver were chased or engraved into Renaissance-type designs of elaborate scroll-

33. Gold tiara in repoussée 'Renaissance' design, English or French, 1850–60.

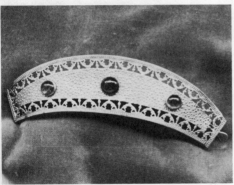

34. Gilt metal barrette with amethyst paste cabochons in the 'Renaissance' style, English, 1865–80.

work, foliate motifs, or niello decoration (figs. 32, 33, 34 and 36). There were hair accessories with a distinct gothic flavour, and Berlin-iron hair ornaments also had their Gothic phase (figs. 35 and 37), after which the fashion for this material died out. During the 1840s there was a fondness for 'historical' coiffures with fanciful names. In these, the chignon was pierced by long pins in the form of arrows and daggers, and the forehead traversed by bandeaux of steel, gold, or jet.

Floral and other naturalistic forms were widely used throughout the whole of Victoria's long reign. A set of diamond jewellery incorporating a design of oak leaves with

23

35. Gilt-metal tiara comb in the Gothic taste c.1855–65.

36. Comb in gilt brass with niello decoration in 'Renaissance' style, English or French, 1840–55.

37. Berlin-iron 'Gothic' tiara comb, probably English, c.1840–55.

acorns demonstrates that this influence permeated even primary jewellery (figs. 38 and 39). The craft of gem-cutting had made great technical advances since the 18th century, with a method similar to the modern brilliant cut being used for the stones in diamond jewellery. This enabled the fire and brilliance of the gem to be displayed to full advantage. There had also been great progress in the arts of gem-setting and mounting, resulting in many exquisite headpieces like the one illustrated here. An increasing amount of primary jewellery could be taken apart, and the components re-assembled in various ways.

From the late 1840s onwards several important influences came to bear upon jewellery design, and therefore upon hair accessories. One of these was a vogue for 'archaeological' styles in ornament, which lasted until the 1880s. Various important excavations during the 19th century led to an interest in, and a taste for, jewellery in the Assyrian, Egyptian, Etruscan and Greek styles. The headband in fig. 40 is an ornament in the Assyrian taste, in silver-gilt. It has a central disc, showing some king or god enthroned, and is surrounded by overlapping metal scales. However, the archaeological taste is not often so obvious in hair accessories, and is more usually represented by motifs such as scarabs, lotus flowers, masks or amphorae. The classical Greek key appears in hair accessories throughout the period, in such widely diverse mediums as enamel, cut-steel, and piqué (figs. 56, 59).

A second important influence which affected hair accessories from the 1840s was the Algerian or Moorish. In the early 1840s the French–Algerian Wars led to an interest in Moorish art, and this is strongly reflected in the design of comb-headings and hairpins until about 1875. The Crimean War further helped to popularize Turkish and Oriental designs in Britain. Motifs such as the Algerian knot, looped chains, tassels and curiously-shaped pendants appear in the so-called *Peigne*

38. *(above)* Case for a set of diamond jewellery, showing fittings for combs, tiara and a brooch, English, 1840–50.

39. *(below)* Diamond tiara assembled from the three brooches in the case (fig. 38), on the gold wirework frame.

*d'Alger.* This type of comb had a heading formed as a series of arches or elaborate piercings, or was looped with an intricate arrangement of chains, each terminating in a tassel, or pendant of filigree, gold or pearls (fig. 41). These pendants hung down over the chignon, and swung as the wearer moved. Other combs, hairpins and bandeaux were given the Moorish flavour by interlaced ornament, arabesques, or pseudo-Arabic script in niello-work (fig. 42).

Niello is a technique of metal decoration somewhat similar to enamel, and was ideally suited for ornaments in the Algerian, Renaissance, and Gothic tastes. The niello, a black metallic substance, was applied to the engraved metal surface and fused into it by means of heat, to form the design. Along with these Algerian-style combs, elaborate gold, silver or pinchbeck hairpins in the Moorish taste were worn from about 1845–65. They were provided in pairs, and had long drops of gold, coral or pearls, or pseudo-Arabic coins hanging from them (fig. 43). They were worn at the back of the head, fixed into the chignon and projecting somewhat, so that the pendants hung free.

A third influence evident in mid-Victorian

40. Silver-gilt headband in the 'Assyrian' style, English *c.*1840–55.

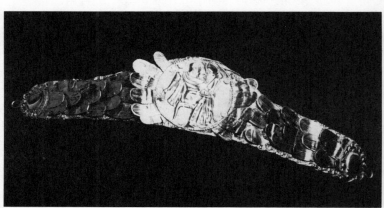

jewellery and ornaments is that of increased travel, which was becoming easier for the prosperous middle-classes. These early tourists returned from Europe with souvenirs of cameos and coral, while from further afield in the Orient came ornaments of ivory and filigree. It is this fondness for collecting in faraway places which explains the presence of so much European and Oriental jewellery in this country today.

Coral, highly-prized throughout most of the Victorian period, was one of the materials imported from Italy in great quantity. Varying in colour from pale pink to deep red (the shade preferred by the Victorians), it was made into a wide range of jewellery and head accessories. Coral could either be carved, or left in its natural branch-like state. In this latter form it was made into tiaras and comb-mounts (fig. 44), often with the addition of berries in coral, gold or pearls. Even more desirable were ornaments featuring coral that had been carved, and these are much sought after by collectors today. The favourite forms were those of acorns, rosebuds, leaf-sprays (fig. 45), fruit or cameos. These elements were mounted into gold or pinchbeck to form tiaras or the headings of combs.

41. Backcomb in the 'Algerian' fashion, gilt-brass with looped chains and pearl drops, English, 1860–75.

42. (*left*) Close-up of 'Algerian' style comb heading, showing niello design with pseudo-Arabic script, 1855–65.

43. (*below*) 'Algerian' style hairpin, one of a pair, with pseudo-Arabic coins, French, 1840–60.

44. Back-comb with heading of red branch coral, English, 1860–80.

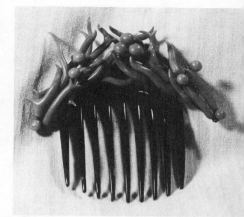

45. Carved coral comb in flower and leaf design, English *c.* 1840–55.

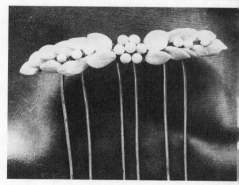

During the 19th century, cameos cut from the shells of the helmet or queen conch were imported in bulk into this country from Rome and Naples. They were mounted in England, the cheaper quality in gilt or pinchbeck frames, and the finer in gold. Five or seven oval cameos, usually graduated in size, might be set into the arched band of a tiara, linked by scrollwork or foliate motifs (fig. 46). A smaller number, usually three, would form the heading of a backcomb (fig. 47). Most of these head

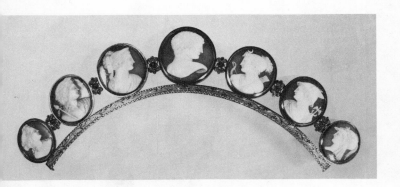

ornaments with cameos originally would have been part of a larger parure. Various other materials, including coral, ivory, lava and jet (fig. 48), were also carved into cameos, although hair accessories featuring these are rarer. There were also cameos of moulded glass and Wedgwood jasperware, which 19th century ingenuity supplied for those with less ample purses.

Moving somewhat further afield, ivory is one of the traditional materials associated

46. Gold tiara with graduated shell cameos, French 1840–60.

47. Gold comb set with three portrait cameos, English or French 1840–60.

48. Tortoiseshell chignon ornament with elaborate arrangement of looped chains, and six jet cameos, English, 1860–75.

49. *(below)* Pierced ivory comb, Chinese workmanship, 1880–90.

with comb-making, and many attractive examples of the ornamental variety found their way into Britain in the second half of the 19th century. Most decorative ivory combs were produced in China for the European market, and were carved into openwork with such Oriental designs as phoenixes, dragons, chrysanthemums, and so on (fig. 49). The ornaments were frequently made in sets, a large backcomb with two matching sidecombs in a complementary design.

In 1876 Queen Victoria was declared Empress of India, thus stimulating a passion for Indian arts and crafts. Combs of carved ivory were among the items produced, and a motif often found in this Indian work is a lotus flower. Hair accessories in elaborate and delicate filigree work were also imported from India in the 1880s, some being enriched with enamel, pearls or turquoise (fig. 50). Closer to home, we find that Queen Victoria's passion for Scotland began a vogue for the traditional gemstones of that country – cairngorms,

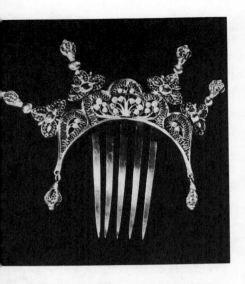

amethysts, agates, and variously coloured
marbles. Although few Scottish hair ornaments as such seem to have been produced,
many show the popular use of agates or
amethysts (fig. 108), or feature the thistle
design (fig. 64).

By the 1860s fashionable jewellery had become massive in size, and highly ornate, in
keeping with the increasing width of the crino-
line and the popularity of heavy, brightly-
coloured fabrics. There was a definite prefer-
ence for strongly-coloured gemstones, and for
a wide range of other materials, such as
mother-of-pearl, jet, tortoiseshell, cut-steel,
and so on. This was also an era of great
technical advances in the applied arts, so that
even the cheapest ornaments were well made
by modern standards. Despite this, no really
new styles evolved, and the archaeological and
Algerian influences continued, in watered-
down forms, into the 1880s.

Female hairstyles were also increasing in
complexity, with great quantities of false hair

52. Comb of the *Peigne Josephine* type with large knobs, gold inlay on black enamel, 1860–75.

53. Tortoiseshell and fire-gilt brass chignon comb, with cornelian and mother-of-pearl cabochons, English, 1860–75.

being used. The coiffure was drawn back into a great chignon, and its importance encouraged the wearing of hair accessories of all kinds (figs. 51 and 54). By day, the chignon was often held in a net of wide mesh, sewn with beads of coral, steel or jet, and kept in place by a large backcomb of tortoiseshell, metal or horn. A popular design was the *Peigne Josephine* which was decorated along the heading with a row of graduated knobs in cut-jet, tortoiseshell, coral, pearls or enamel (fig. 52). Others had a series of large semi-precious stones, usually amethysts, garnets, agates or cornelians, set into oval mounts on a raised gallery (figs. 53, 108). Although cut-steel work gradually declined in quality throughout the 19th century, there were still some fine, if rather ornate, pieces being made in the middle of Victoria's reign. An attractive motif was that of wheat-ears (fig. 55), although stars, butterflies, scrollwork, encrusted rosettes and the Greek-key (fig. 56), are also found in this work. Most attractive are those ornaments in which the steels are combined with other materials, such as mother-of-pearl or jet (fig. 57).

From about 1860 these decorative combs became more sophisticated in design. Many

54. Gold hairpin set with an oval topaz, 1860–70.

55. *(below)* Steel comb with pendant drop in wheat-ears design, English, 1865–75.

56. Cut-steel comb with Greek key and star design, English, 1860–80.

57. Tiara of arcaded design in cut-steel with jet, English, 1840–60.

were provided with a metal hinge which enabled the heading to rotate (fig. 58). The presence of this hinge usually indicates a date from the second half of the 19th century, and in some examples it will rotate through a full 180 degrees. This permitted the ornament to be worn in a number of ways: as a conventional backcomb, within the chignon, or above the forehead as a diadem. In these examples, both teeth and heading would be gently curved, giving a comfortable and secure fit to the head.

By the second half of the 19th century

combs and hair accessories were being mass-produced by factories all over the country, and the handcrafting of them was a dying art. One such factory, the Aberdeen Comb Works, had no fewer than 612 patterns in production for ladies' braid combs. The extent of the mass-production explains why hair ornaments have survived in such profusion and variety, and the collector will seldom come across two identical ones, unless they were intended as a pair.

From the late 1860s the observance of mourning became increasingly important as a social custom. In such circumstances, only the most sombre jewels could be worn, such as those in onyx, piqué (fig. 59), or jet. However, most of these so-called 'jet' hair ornaments are really made from French jet, a glittering form of black glass. This is a very different substance from the genuine Whitby jet (fig. 48), although nevertheless, most attractive in appearance. It became high fashion in the

59. Dark tortoiseshell comb with silver piqué inlay in Greek key pattern, English, 1875–85.

60. French jet ornaments: star pin (*left*), hair prong (*centre*), and crescent aigrette (*right*), English, 1870–90.

1870s, and sets of hairpins, from two to six in number, might be made as stars, flowers, butterflies or crescents, and scattered about the evening coiffure (fig. 60). At this period also, the increasing height of hairstyles brought the aigrette back into favour. Those in cut-jet, taking the form of a sword, flower-spray or crescent were particularly favoured (fig. 60, *right* and *centre*).

Another hair accessory which came into prominence at this time was the barrette or hairslide. In the late 1870s a popular coiffure was the 'Catogan', a low style, with a plait or twisted braid caught on the nape. In order to hold the Catogan, a large clasp or barrette was used. Most of these 19th century barrettes take the form of a rectangular or crescent-shaped plaque in metal, horn or tortoiseshell, adorned with the same range of materials as are found in other accessories (fig. 34). After about 1870 hair accessories in metal decorated with stones ceased to be fashionable for a while, and were replaced by those in carved and pierced tortoiseshell (fig. 61). The blond variety, which is the colour of amber, was the shade preferred. The first performance of the opera *Carmen* in 1875 was followed by a vogue for high Spanish combs in carved and pierced

61. Barrette in openwork blond tortoiseshell, 1890–1900.

tortoiseshell (fig. 62).

During the 1880s the use of false hair gradually decreased. The coiffure became less elaborate, and its accessories smaller and simpler. A reaction set in against the heavy, ornate jewellery that had been used for the last twenty years. In the new lighter jewellery the preferred gemstones were South African diamonds, which were imported in quantity from the 1880s onwards. Such was the immense popularity of diamonds that from 1890 almost

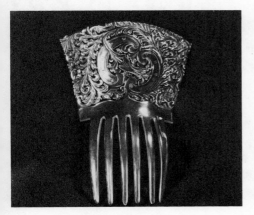

62. Spanish-style comb in pierced blond tortoiseshell, 1870–85.

**63.** Tortoiseshell backcomb with simple pearl decoration, 1880–90.

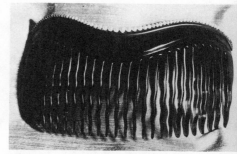

**64.** Scottish thistle silver hairpin with turquoise (*left*), and gold-headed 'Etruscan' hairpin (*right*), 1890–1900.

all coloured stones were banished from fashionable wear and only the paler stones such as pearls, opals and moonstones, were considered suitable substitutes.

Ornamental haircombs at this period became smaller and simpler in form. They were generally decorated with a single row of diamonds, turquoises or pearls (fig. 63) across the heading, or with metal openwork (fig. 64, *right*). A favourite of the year 1890 was the Galatea, which had three or five radiating stalks, each tipped with a jewel (fig. 65, *left*).

65. Combs of carved and faceted amber in Galatea (*left*), and floral (*right*) designs, 1880–90.

66. Floral design comb, set with garnets, English, 1880–90.

Bohemian garnets, also fashionable in the 1880s, were featured in some attractive small combs and pins of encrusted star or flower designs (fig. 66). Another attractive material which enjoyed a brief popularity in the 1880s was amber, particularly attractive when both clear and clouded varieties were combined in the same piece (fig. 65, *right*).

Hairpins, particularly in sets, appeared in all the foregoing materials and designs. During the 1890s there was a fondness for such sentimental motifs as lover's knots, hearts (fig.

39

67. *(above)* Foliate design diamond comb-mount showing the 1890s tendency towards height.

68. *(above right)* Sentimental motifs of the 1890s: star-shaped hairpin, silver and paste (*left*), heart-shaped olivines encircled by pearls (*centre*), and gold lover's knot (*right*).

69. Aigrette headdress, sequinned gauze wings, with feathers in shades of green and gold, 1890–1900. Ornaments of this nature were favoured by younger women.

68), butterflies and flowers. However, the favourite design was that of a star, in diamonds, pearls or paste (fig. 68), and a number of these might be scattered about the evening coiffure. At the turn of the century the aigrette, particularly in diamonds, was one of the most important hair accessories (fig. 67). Small ostrich feathers in black, white or delicate colours to tone with the gown were often introduced as a background to the glittering gems.

For those women who could not afford diamonds, there were similar ornaments in moonstones, half-pearls or pastes. There were also attractive fabric accessories in the form of spangled gauze wings (fig. 69), tulle poufs, flower sprays, and upstanding bows with diamanté or sequin embroidery. Head ornaments of this type were favoured by young ladies, for there was again a convention that expensive diamond jewellery should be reserved for married women. Most young girls therefore wore only flowers or light ornaments with evening dress.

# 3.  Art Nouveau to Art Deco, 1900–1940

70.  Diamond coronet of flower design, and diamond tiara/necklace with star motifs, *c.*1890–1900.

THE hairstyles of the Edwardian period were characterized by an appearance of soft fullness, the hair being dressed over pads to give it width. At this time, the tiara was the headdress selected by most prosperous fashionable women on formal occasions. A stickler for correct dress, Edward VII once rebuked a society lady for appearing with a diamond crescent in her hair, rather than the regulation tiara! For those who could afford them diamonds were the gemstones invariably chosen, and platinum was the preferred metal for settings. The designs used in such tiaras were often somewhat conventional – delicate scrollwork, or floral patterns in openwork settings. Another popular design was a series of stars which could be separated for alternative wear as hairpins, pendants or brooches. Most primary jewellery of the period is composite in this way, and many diamond necklaces were provided with a framework upon which they could be fastened for alternative wear as a tiara (fig. 70). There were also comb-fittings, which enabled a pendant, brooch or other ornament to be worn in the hair (fig. 71).

71.  Tortoiseshell and gold fitting to which a brooch or pendant may be attached for wear in the hair, *c.*1900.

72. Diamond aigrette in the form of a star with stones on 'knife-edge' wires, contemporary photograph, c.1900–05.

The passion for aigrettes continued for some years into the new century; they were primarily set with diamonds, although often combined with pearls, opals or turquoises. The main purpose in all this diamond jewellery was to concentrate attention upon the beauty of the gemstones, and to keep their settings as inconspicuous as possible. To this effect, the stones were often mounted upon 'knife-edge' wires. In this method, a strip of metal was hammered paper thin, and then attached with the narrow edge facing the front of the ornament. The diamonds mounted upon this almost-invisible strip of metal thus appeared to hover above the wearer's head without support, giving a very delicate effect. Many of these aigrettes were also made *tremblant*, and two of the favourite themes were wings and stars (fig. 72). In other aigrettes the designs are based on flower-sprays, feathers or crescents.

73. Gold and pearl butterfly *tremblant* hairpin (*centre*), with star hairpins in moonstones and pastes, 1895–1905.

For those whose purses would not extend to tiaras or important aigrettes, there were diamond stars, crescents, bows, flowers, butterflies and swords to enliven the evening dressing (fig. 74). These designs were also imitated in pearls, moonstones and pastes (fig. 73). Such decorations might be worn in sets, or alone, as the base of an upstanding ornament in gauze, tulle, or ostrich feathers. There was a feeling of height to the current accessories, and also of lightness and glitter. Young girls customarily chose lighter ornaments, such as flower-sprays or coronets (fig. 75), a gauze bow or wings, or small ostrich tips. As the 20th century advanced, these accessories made from fabrics, beads and feathers were to become even more fashionable. Unfortunately, they were of a less durable nature than their counterparts in metal and tortoiseshell, and comparatively few have survived in good condition.

The vogue for colourless stones and inconspicuous settings existed alongside the distinctive arts and crafts and art nouveau jewellery, with its emphasis on exotic designs and materials. The Arts and Crafts movement was an attempt to reject the mechanical and vulgar

74. *(above)* Sword-shaped hair prong set with diamonds, *c.*1900.

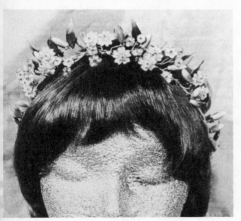

75. *(left)* Floral wreath in hand-tinted blown-glass, 1900–10.

43

76. Enamel and silver Arts and Crafts style hair comb, showing the strong Celtic influence of much British work, 1890–1905.

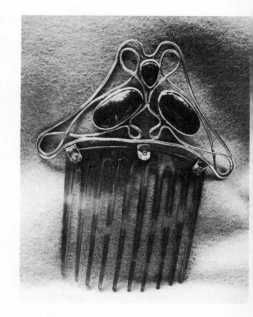

77. *(below)* Horn comb set with cornelian and mother-of-pearl, 1900–05.

commercialism which affected the applied arts in the late 19th century, and to return to the medieval ideal. This ideal was that an article should be both designed and made by the same craftsman, using traditional methods. In practice, however, many of the arts and crafts ornaments produced in this country lack the finish and sophistication of Continental art nouveau work. They were often made by amateurs who lacked professional training, and much British work has a rather naive appearance (fig. 77).

The materials used were modest too, silver being the metal almost invariably chosen. It was set with semi-precious stones such as opals, turquoises, cornelians and moonstones. These gems were usually presented as cabochons – polished in spherical form – rather than being cut into facets (fig. 78), and were combined with baroque and blister

78. Horn comb with a heading of swirled silver leaves enclosing chrysoprase cabochons, c.1900–05.

pearls, and such inexpensive materials as coral, mother-of-pearl, and horn. The designs were also austere, and many jewels were Celtic in feeling (fig. 76).

From about 1895 the tiara was strongly affected by the art nouveau movement, and many experimental forms appeared (fig. 79).

79. Tiara of enamelled gold ivy leaves alternating with fruits of chrysoprase, by Giuliano of London, after 1896.

80. *(above)* Butterfly hair ornament in *plique à jour* enamel, gold, and diamonds. French, *c.*1900.

81. *(above right)* Carved and tinted dragonfly horn comb, English, *c.*1900–05.

82. *(below)* Carved horn and opal comb in the form of stylized seaweed, by Lucien Gaillard, French, *c.*1900.

However, the most sympathetic interpretations of the new style appeared in combs, pins and barrettes. An important feature of many art nouveau hair accessories is the use made of different enamel techniques to enliven the design. A particularly effective technique which appears most frequently in Continental work is *plique à jour*. In this method, the backing-plate is removed after firing, so that the enamel remains transparent like a stained-glass window. *Plique à jour* appears at its most spectacular in hair ornaments because, in wear, the light is able to pass through the enamel and show up the design to greatest advantage. The motifs chosen for this work were mainly taken from nature, such as a butterfly or other insect with outspread wings (fig. 80).

Until the art nouveau period, horn had always been regarded as a comparatively humble material, and had taken second place to tortoiseshell in the manufacture of quality hair ornaments. It is due to the influence of artists like René Lalique and Lucien Gaillard that the great potential of this attractive material was at last realized. Horn is particularly suitable for hair accessories because of its lightness and strength, and also because it is so versatile. It can be carved and tinted to represent a variety of natural things – the translucent wings of insects, the petals of overblown

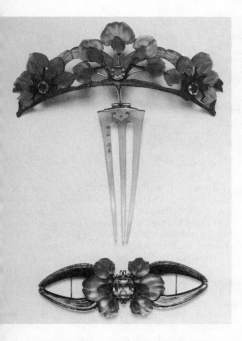

83. Tiara comb and matching buckle in carved horn, overlaid with sweet peas in cast glass, with topaz centres, by René Lalique, c.1903–04.

flowers, or the delicate veining of a leaf. Fig. 81 shows a horn comb in which the material is used to maximum effect to portray a dragonfly in delicate shades of brown and cream. Both Gaillard and Lalique used horn extensively in their comb designs, often combined with gold, gemstones, and various enamel techniques (figs. 82 and 83). The themes they used were mainly inspired by nature – leaves, flowers, and various insects.

A revival of Egyptian motifs in turquoise, enamel and oxidized silver had come about through the success of the play *Cléopatre* in 1890. In this, Sarah Bernhardt wore a number of exotic turquoise ornaments which excited great interest. Again, under the influence of art nouveau, there appeared hair ornaments decorated with turquoise matrix, lapis lazuli

84. Egyptian taste oxydized silver comb with stylized birds whose wings are inlaid with multi-coloured translucent enamels, and turquoise cabochons, c.1895–1900.

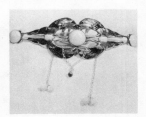

85. Art nouveau motifs translated well into barrettes. These are of beaten copper, decorated with turquoises and agates, French, c.1900.

and enamel, with a distinctly Egyptian feel about them. The large comb in fig. 84 shows four bird figures in oxidized silver, supporting a central turquoise matrix. The birds' wings are in translucent enamels of blue, green and mauve, making this a very vivid ornament.

Towards the end of the 19th century the barrette again became an important adornment, and from 1895 it appeared in metal, tortoiseshell and horn. This form of accessory was particularly well adapted to portray art nouveau designs, as can be seen from the examples in fig. 85. As well as gold and precious metals, such barrettes also appeared

86. Silver hairpins displaying art nouveau influence, Birmingham, 1904–06.

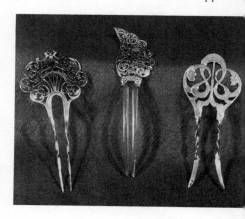

in beaten-copper ornamented with a variety of the cheaper materials, including turquoise, chrysoprase and agate. Ivy and sycamore leaves were popular motifs, together with the curvilinear designs that are typical of art nouveau at its zenith.

Despite the care and craftsmanship that went into most art nouveau ornaments they were never a great economic success in this country. The market for them was simply too restricted. The jewels did not appeal to the social elite, who preferred the more spectacular glitter of diamonds. At the same time, these hand-made pieces were far too expensive for ordinary working people, who continued to buy the cheaper mass-produced wares from Birmingham. Nor were the versatile manufacturers of that city slow in taking up the new style. Great quantities of machine-made silver combs, pins and barrettes were produced in Birmingham between the years 1895 and 1910. Many show unmistakable art nouveau influence in the designs, which are usually naturalistic, asymmetric, or composed of intricate strapwork (fig. 86). It was just this degree of mass-production which vulgarized art nouveau, and by 1910 its short reign was virtually over.

87. Contemporary hairdressing and ornaments. *Hairdressing*, April, 1914.

88. Bandeau ornaments: silver-gilt, mother-of-pearl and agates (*top*), and white metal with diamanté (*bottom*), 1910–15.

89. Headdress of gold lace and artificial pearls in the style of the Russian Ballet, c.1910–20. Although intended for stage use, these headdresses strongly influenced conventional evening wear. (*See* fig. 99.)

From about 1911 fashionable hairdressing began to conform more closely to the shape of the head. The new mode demanded a 'Grecian' dressing, with the hair softly waved into a loose chignon. Along with this Grecian style, the classic bandeau again became modish, and its long reign was to endure for about fifteen years. These bandeaux were produced in a wide range of materials, either in fabric as a dress accessory, or in metal and gemstones as an article of jewellery (figs. 87 and 88). So profound was the influence of this accessory that from about 1913 even the court tiara had grown narrow and ribbonlike, and was being worn low on the brow in a truly classical fashion.

At this time the Oriental theme in costume was very strong, due to the influence of Paul Poiret, whose 'harem' evening dresses were inspired by the costumes of the Russian Ballet. Bandeaux were given the eastern look with tassels, long beaded pendants, or elaborate encrusted embroidery (fig. 89). Again, few of these handsome but fragile accessories have survived, since they were discarded as soon as they grew shabby or the fashion changed. As well as headbands of fabric and beads, there were those in metal, set with jewels or pastes.

90. White metal bandeau ornamented with pastes, c.1915–20. Ornaments of this nature often reveal a taste for the exotic, which affected formal dress at this time.

91. Coronet in French jet 'butterfly' design, 1918–25. Jet was enjoying a renewed vogue at this period.

An ornament of the period 1910–15 in fig. 90 is of silver, adorned with pastes in an elaborate bird design. Others took the form of fanciful crowns (fig. 91), or diamanté flowers, often combined with an upstanding plume at one side.

Many books dealing with costume and jewellery imply that all hair ornaments came to an abrupt end in the early 1920s, due to the almost universal fashion for shingled hair. It is probably truer that the wearing of them declined gradually throughout the post-war period, for not all women had their hair bobbed. Some continued to wear it long, either in a roll, or a chignon on the nape. Even those with shorn locks often added a small false plait or bun for evening wear. Spanish shawls with long fringes became the mode in the early 1920s. They were worn with shoulder-length earrings and large Spanish combs, thrust into the chignon at an acute angle. There is often a geometric feeling about such combs, in keeping with the spirit of art deco. The most common pattern is a fan-shaped design of radiating spokes, often strongly asymmetric (fig. 92).

However, many of these combs were no longer of tortoiseshell, but of celluloid, vul-

92. Two celluloid combs, 1915–25.

51

93. Twenties comb of yellow celluloid with brown stylized flowers.

canite, or one of the other synthetics designed to imitate natural materials. Thus, the story of decorative combs in the 1920s is one of diminishing materials – horn, tortoiseshell and ivory being replaced by man-made substitutes which were not only cheaper, but much more versatile. The use of synthetics for hair accessories began as early as 1869, when Charles Wesley Hyatt of New York invented celluloid (figs. 92, 93). Celluloid was manufactured in this country under the trade name Xylonite and was widely used to simulate tortoiseshell, ivory, amber and other materials in the late 19th and early 20th centuries. However, celluloid was highly inflammable, which caused it to lose ground somewhat when safer materials emerged in the early 20th century.

One such was casein, a plastic made from milk protein. It was frequently left white to simulate ivory, and goods made from it were marketed under the trade name Galalith (fig.

94. Casein (Galalith) combs, imitating ivory *c.*1915–20.

94). Another important early synthetic was vulcanite, pioneered by Charles Goodyear. He discovered that india rubber, after being mixed with sulphur and exposed to a very high temperature, turned into a black horn-like substance. His new discovery was soon being used to produce combs and costume jewellery, and was often used to simulate jet (fig. 95). Until this time, the makers of hair accessories had always been limited as to size and shape by the peculiarities of the various materials used. It was now possible, by means of moulding, to produce combs, barrettes and bandeaux of any required size and design.

With the discovery of synthetics, the use of ivory, tortoiseshell and horn declined rapidly, and the new products had almost entirely superseded natural materials by the end of the 1920s. For some years the high Spanish combs continued in fashion, along with barrettes of 'tortoiseshell', enamel or diamanté, or (fig.

95. Vulcanite comb c.1900.

96. Pair of silver-headed combs with geometric motif c.1915–25.

97. *(above)* Comb with applied multi-coloured feathers, 1918–25.

98. *(below)* Lace bandeau ornament sewn with diamanté and French jet, in the Egyptian style, 1918–25.

96) in geometric or formalized plant designs. Some of these ornaments show distinct Oriental influence in the use of colour or motif. Other combs were given an exotic treatment by applied decoration in lace, flowers, or multi-coloured feathers (fig. 97).

The bandeau was, however, the favourite hair accessory during the early 1920s, usually taking the form of a metal or tortoiseshell ornament, or a low tiara, set with gemstones or pastes. The Egyptian influence had lingered on into art deco, and received fresh impetus from the opening of the tomb of Tutankhamen in 1923. This Egyptian look is strongly reflected in bandeaux which are beaded, encrusted with sequins, or with pastes and cut-jet (fig. 98). Such ornaments sometimes displayed long beaded tassels at each side, or several ropes of pearls or diamanté passing beneath the chin from one side to another (fig.

99). These however were extreme styles, worn only by ultra-fashionable women.

The bandeau in its various forms retained favour until about 1925, when the boyish 'shingle' came into vogue. Almost overnight hair accessories of all types, even bandeaux, disappeared completely from the pages of fashion magazines, and their place was taken by long dangling earrings in geometric designs. However, by 1930 the hair was becoming longer at the sides, and the back sometimes grown long enough to be formed into a small roll or bunch of curls. By the early 1930s hairdressers and fashion writers were making strenuous efforts to re-introduce hair accessories into evening dress.

In this they had some partial success. To hold the growing side-locks small diamanté or enamel barrettes were used, following the same geometric designs as in the 1920s. Few

99. *(above)* Black velvet tiara with diamanté embroidery and 'chinstrap', 1920–25. An example of the quasi-oriental headdresses favoured by ultra-fashionable women.

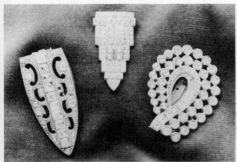

100. *(left)* Paste dress clips in geometric designs were often pressed into service as hair decorations in the 1930s.

101. White metal tiara with French paste, 1930–35.

102. Diamond necklace, c.1935. The centre portion may be detached for wear as a tiara.
103. *(below)* Alice band in transparent plastic, with diamanté, 1930–35.

hair accessories as such were being produced, and so paste dress clips were often pressed into service to act as barrettes and clasps (fig. 100). Small decorative combs with diamanté tops held the growing ends of hair at the nape, and the tiara made a re-appearance on formal occasions (figs. 101, 102). A fashion that was re-introduced in the early 1930s was the Alice-band. This might be made of anything from metal to gaily coloured or transparent plastic, decorated with pearls, rhinestones or open-work (fig. 103). It was in accessories and costume ornaments of this kind that plastics were first used as decorative media in their own right, rather than simply to imitate materials like amber and tortoiseshell.

Another attractive headdress introduced about 1935 was the Juliet cap, a small skull-cap designed to fit closely to the crown of the head. For evening it might be made from some rich fabric to match the gown, or was sequin-ned and embroidered. Another idea was to have a network composed entirely of pearls,

small beads or diamanté (fig. 104). In 1937 the upswept Edwardian style, with curls piled high on the crown of the head, came into vogue. For evening wear, these upswept styles, and the elaborate rolls of the early 1940s, were held with small combs and slides in plastic and diamanté. However, short hairstyles again returned in the mid-1940s, and this discouraged the wearing of decorative accessories. To some extent, their place was taken by the hats which were customarily worn to early evening functions in the 1950s and 1960s. Despite the efforts of hairdressers and fashion writers, the taste for decorative hair accessories did not really re-establish itself until comparatively recent years (figs. 105 and 106).

104. *(above)* Juliet cap of openwork diamanté mesh, 1930–40.

105. *(left)* Handmade gilt metal hairpin, American manufacture, 1982.

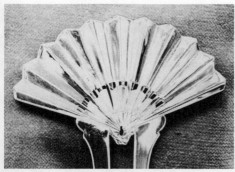

106. Modern hair comb in moulded glass and diamanté. The leaf motifs may be bent to various angles. Ken Lane, Burlington Arcade.

# 4.

# Collecting

**P**ROBABLY the first advice that should be given to a new collector in any field is to learn as much as possible about styles, materials and techniques before parting with cash. Collectors who choose a narrow field and then research it thoroughly will often find themselves at a decided advantage when rummaging through the junk at fleamarkets. Until quite recently, combs and hair accessories were among the Cinderellas of the antiques world – out of favour, and sometimes available for the equivalent of a few pence! However, now that hair ornaments are again in fashion, they are being sought out, not only by collectors, but by those who wish to use them for their original purpose of decorating the hair. Compared with modern chain-store goods, which are often of flimsy quality, genuine old ornaments can represent very good value.

It is difficult to be specific about the prices one should expect to pay for hair accessories, since they are often either over or under-priced by dealers who know little about them. Prices can range from a pound or two for simple pins, barrettes and combs in early synthetics up to

107. Floral design comb-mount in the form of marguerites, white enamel with topaz centres, 1860–75, worth about £50.

108. Tortoiseshell and gold chignon comb set with agates, 1860–75, worth about £120.

five-figure sums for important gemstone pieces. It is often the ornaments that are less wearable today, such as large ornate combs and diadems of the Victorian period, that can represent the greatest bargains. These are sometimes available for little more than the intrinsic value of their materials (figs. 107 and 108).

The best places to search for hair accessories are antique fairs and markets, particularly the larger fleamarkets and the London street stalls. Junk stalls, jumbles, and second-hand shops can all yield surprising finds, while any shop dealing in antique jewellery, small collectors' items or costume is worth an enquiry. There are also specialist auctions in jewellery, art nouveau, and costume held at the larger salerooms, and these may well include one or two hair accessories.

In my experience, hair accessories have been less subject to deliberate counterfeiting than other jewellery. They were out of fashion for many years, so that imitating them was simply not worth while. This does not mean that the collector is immune from dishonesty.

109. Rear view of hairpin converted from an old filigree buckle.

Perhaps the easiest form of deceit is the temptation to 'improve' plain tortoiseshell or horn ornaments by sticking on loose decorations. When a decorative element was applied to a tortoiseshell comb or pin, the method was to attach it with small metal rivets, which should be clearly visible on the back. If these are not present, the decorations were probably stuck on with epoxy to make the piece seem more desirable.

I have also experienced some elaborate haircombs that were 'made up' from headings and comb-mounts which obviously did not begin life together. A mid-Victorian style heading might be attached to a turn-of-the-century comb of blond horn. In other cases, the headings were obviously parts of old buckles (fig. 109), necklaces or brooches that had been re-mounted as combs. Sometimes the result is an attractive ornament, but the customer ought to know what is being paid for. Again, the clue lies in the attaching rivets. In the original state these would match the metal heading in colour, and in ornaments of gold or silver would probably be of the same. A delicate cresting of precious metal that is attached with clumsy pins of base metal may well indicate an amateur restoration.

Another question which baffles many people is how to distinguish real tortoiseshell from clever imitations. The two materials have a completely different 'feel', which one can come to recognize with practice, and tortoiseshell is often the heavier. Generally, plastic has more flexibility than shell, and the prongs of a synthetic comb will have a certain amount of 'give' not present in real shell. The most reliable test is to file the piece in an unobtrusive place with a metal nail-file. A synthetic will give off the unmistakable smell of burnt plastic.

There remains the difficult question of whether damaged pieces should be purchased. The replacing of gemstones in expensive ornaments should always be entrusted to a jeweller specializing in antique repairs. However, one should bear in mind that professional repairs can prove expensive, and may well come to more than the original cost if an imperfect piece is bought cheaply. Damaged enamel is impossible to repair properly, without stripping and re-firing the piece, and is best passed over. Early paste ornaments in which the metal foils have greatly discoloured, or cut-steel which is badly rusted or missing its rivets should likewise be rejected.

However, there are instances when amateur restorers can come into their own. Fragile beaded, embroidered or sequinned ornaments are often found in a bedraggled condition. Likewise, seed-pearl ornaments are rarely in perfect order, as the thread holding them to the mother-of-pearl backing will have become brittle over the years. Nowadays, it is almost impossible to find anyone willing to undertake this tedious restoration. If the collector has the necessary patience and skill to do the work, then a rare and delicate ornament might well be rescued and restored.

110. Silver and paste 'loop' pin, mounted on hinged prongs which enable it to be bent to the shape of the head, 1890–1910.

61

# Books for Further Reading

Clifford, A. *Cut Steel and Berlin Iron Jewellery*, Adams and Dart, 1971.
Corson, R. *Fashions in Hair*, Peter Owen, 1965.
De Cortais, G. *Women's Headdress and Hairstyles*, Batsford, 1973.
Flower, M. *Victorian Jewellery*, Cassell, 1951.
Hague, N. 'Nineteenth Century Hair Ornaments', *Antique Collecting*, March, 1980.
—— 'Ornamental Haircombs, 1780–1880', *Costume*, 1982.
—— 'Twentieth Century Hair Ornaments', *Antique Collecting*, April, 1981.
Holme, C. (Editor). *Modern Design in Jewellery and Fans*, Studio, 1902.
Rhodes, A. 'Jewellery to Adorn the Hair', *Antique Dealer and Collector's Guide*, June, 1979.
Vever, H. *La Bijouterie Française au XIXe Siècle*, Paris, 1908.

## Contemporary Periodicals

*Ackermann's Repository* 1809–1828; *La Belle Assemblée* 1807–1855; *Englishwoman's Domestic Magazine* 1860–1876; *Le Follet* 1845–1860; *Hairdresser's Chronicle and Trade Journal* 1866–1928; *Lady's Magazine* 1770–1815; *Moniteur de la Coiffure* 1874–1900; *The Queen* 1869–1940; *Vogue* 1916–1940; *World of Fashion* 1827–1850.

# Where Hair Accessories May Be Seen

Museum of Costume, Bath.
City Museum and Art Gallery, Birmingham.
British Museum (The Hull–Grundy Gift), London.
Museum of London, London.
Victoria and Albert Museum, London.
Gallery of English Costume, Platt Hall, Manchester.
National Museum of Hairdressing, Carlett Park Technical College, Eastham, Wirral (appointment necessary).
Castle Museum, York

Not all these museums have the collections on display, so it is advisable to enquire before visiting.

# Acknowledgements

The author and publishers would like to thank the following for permission to use the photographs in this book:
Birmingham City Museum and Art Gallery 15, 18; British Museum, Hull Grundy Gift 2, 5, 6, 7, 25, 38, 39, 79; Castle Museum, York 37; Messrs Sotheby's 4, 11, 29, 35, 68, 70, 74, 80, 82, 102; Victoria and Albert Museum, Crown Copyright 83; Wedgwood Museum, Barlaston 9; the remaining items are taken from private collections and were photographed by Eric Shenton and Peter Bate, to whom the author is particularly grateful.

# Index

Bold page numbers refer to illustrations